CHARTING THE COURSE

A JOURNEY INTO
GENEROUS AND ABUNDANT LIVING

Written By

Rev. Dr. Tyler Kaufmann

FREEDOM RINGERS

PUBLISHING

Copyright Page

ISBN: 979-8-9988808-1-0 (Paperback)

Cover design by: Freedom Ringers Publishing
Printed in the United States of America

Scripture quotations unless otherwise noted are from the **New International Version (NIV)**.

The stories and experiences shared in this book are true to the best of the author's recollection. In some cases, minor details have been adjusted for clarity, anonymity, and readability, but the essence and meaning remain faithful to the events as they occurred. Any resemblance to individuals beyond those explicitly mentioned is purely coincidental.

This book explores biblical narratives and themes through interpretation and reflection. The insights, metaphors, and perspectives presented are intended to deepen engagement with Scripture, not to alter its historical or spiritual significance.

DEDICATION

To my **Aunt Tammy and Uncle Scott Stuhr**—thank you for the cousins' campouts on the lake. As a kid, I loved those times; only now do I realize the breadth of the gift they were—the generous sacrifices of your time, the opportunities you set aside to "get ahead," the resources you freely shared, and the outdoor wisdom you poured into each of us. You gave us more than adventures—you gave us each other. Those campouts made my cousins feel like brothers and sisters, and I am forever grateful for the example you set of giving your lives away for others.

To my **parents, Pete and Sherri Kaufmann**—in family road trips you not only carried me across this great country and taught me to love the outdoors, but also how to immerse myself in local life wherever I go, and to live generously. Dad, your gratitude and zest for life shows me how to give freely while stewarding resources wisely. Mom, your joy in creating things and finding hidden treasures or just the right gift has taught me that generosity transforms not only the one who receives, but also the one who gives as well.

Because of you four, this journey—and the lessons within it—had a starting point long before I ever put words on paper.

HOW TO USE THIS DEVOTIONAL

This devotional is designed to help you *cultivate a generous spirit and live more abundantly as a result*. Each week offers an opportunity to reflect and renew your spirit. Whether you're moving through this study on your own or with others, here's how to get the most out of your journey.

1. Read the Charting the Course and Frontloading sections.

2. Reflect with the **Daily Devotionals**

    Each day, you'll find a brief reflection and a Scripture reading, along with a reflection prompt. These daily touchpoints are meant to stir your soul and open you to the voice of God.

3. Revisit the Week with the **Small Group Guide**

    At the end of each week, you'll find a short guide to help you process and apply what you've experienced. You can use this guide in a group, with a friend, or as a solo time of deeper reflection.

The ability to live more abundantly expands when we daily practice giving and receiving.

Table of Contents

CHARTING THE COURSE

The call to venture into wild places comes in many forms. Some are drawn by alpine summits and desert mesas, others by winding rivers or dense forests. Whatever the terrain, the pull is rarely about utility—it's about discovery, beauty, and the sheer joy of testing our limits in creation.

The French alpinist Lionel Terray once called climbers "conquistadors of the useless," a phrase Yvon Chouinard loved to repeat about climbing and surfing: you pour out sweat and strength for something that—at least in practical terms—doesn't accomplish anything. You reach the top of a peak and discover nothing more than a view waiting there. You could have walked up from another easier direction and captured that, but you didn't, you chose the more difficult way. Why? Because the point is not the summit—it's the way you traveled to get there.

In the world of wilderness navigation, "charting the course" is the art of planning your way forward—studying maps, tracing ridgelines, marking valleys, noting river crossings, and preparing for both the predictable, as well as the unexpected. Backpackers, climbers, paddlers and mountaineers all do it before they set foot on the trail or launch onto the water. You don't chart a course so you can race to the end—you do it so you can be fully alive, alert, and attentive along the way.

This devotional is about that kind of stewardship. Not a pressured march toward a financial summit, but a spiritual trek where every step has value. The goal isn't to measure speed or status, but to notice how God meets you on the trail—through fears faced, provisions provided, gratitude given, and courage discovered. Charting the course of generosity means preparing not only to reach the mountaintop, but to travel with joy, to share the road with others, and to glimpse God's abundance in every step.

That's why I've chosen this metaphor to guide our journey together. Outdoor navigation offers a way of seeing stewardship not as a burden or a ledger, but as an invitation into adventure. My prayer is that as you travel these pages, you'll discover that the path of generosity is less about arriving at some grand destination and more about learning to move freely, faithfully, and fully with God along the way—and come alive as a result.

FRONTLOADING THE JOURNEY

In the field of outdoor recreation leadership, there is a powerful tool used called *frontloading*. It's the art of preparing hearts and priming minds for the journey ahead—setting expectations and sharing the "why" behind the way a group will operate. Before you set out—whether it's a mountaineering expedition, a long hike, or a whitewater rafting trip—you take time to set expectations and explain not only what you'll do, but the "why" behind *the way* you'll do it. That clarity keeps people from going rogue and helps each person see their role in making the whole operation work.

When the ascent is steep, the route uncertain, or the weather unpredictable, people don't only need instructions—they need perspective. They need to know why they're pacing themselves, why they're keeping a certain formation, or why they're carrying particular items. A shared sense of purpose holds a team together when fatigue sets in or the unexpected happens. It builds morale, keeps people engaged, and transforms a group of those "just getting through," into a team.

The following chapter is our frontloading for the generosity trail we are about to walk together. Before we take the first step, it's worth pausing to remember why we're here, what we're aiming for, and how the journey will shape us. Knowing the why will help us keep going when the trail feels long, the climb grows steep, or the "view" is hidden in the clouds. It's what will keep us moving in the same direction—trusting that what we're doing matters, and that we'll see the fruit of it in God's time.

THE POWER OF GENEROUS LIVING

WHY BE GENEROUS?

Most people don't start with a spiritual treatise on how to use their time and money to glorify God; they start with questions like: *What does the Creator of the universe need with my resources? What's the point—and does this actually help me, my family, and the world?* If giving doesn't make sense on Monday afternoon or help us raise our kids well, why would we do it?

This devotional keeps inviting us to ask another question as well. It's a simple prayer:

"Lord, where would You have me be in my giving and in my living?"

We don't ask it to check a religious box. We ask it to grow as bearers of the **imago Dei**—the image of the God who delights to give. We ask the question because we believe we are God's beloved and following God's ways are good for us.

Pastors speak to this in various ways. Adam Hamilton calls generosity a path to joy and contentment that pushes back on fear and the consumer script of "more." Tom Berlin calls it defying the cultural gravity that keeps pulling our hearts toward accumulation and away from freedom. Leonard Sweet suggests generosity is a sign that makes the gospel visible. And Andy Stanley reminds us that the issue isn't wealth; it's where we place our trust, our allegiance. Their point is the same:

generosity isn't a tax; it's *a way of becoming more of who God intended us to be*—it's a practice that forms us into people who participate in God's creative, redemptive work with our time, talents, money, and presence. That's the theological "why."

Of course, we don't have to take the theological 'why' on faith alone—research attests to the practical 'how.' Study after study shows the measureable ways generosity reshapes our lives, families, and communities. Theology gives us the vision; research confirms the fruit. Again and again, generosity proves to form us, heal us, and even rewire us for joyful, abundant living.

WHAT THE RESEARCH KEEPS FINDING

- **Well-being & happiness.** People who give time and money report higher life satisfaction. Over the long run, generous people show better mental and physical health—and even longer lifespans.[1]

- **Kindness is healthy.** Harvard researchers note that acts of kindness are associated with improved mood, lower anxiety, and stronger connection with others. And those connections themselves predict better health.[2]

- **Spending on others works.** Across cultures, experiments show that giving to others increases happiness—especically when people can see the impact of their gift.[3]

- **Faith and community.** Research shows that people who are active in faith communities are more likely to volunteer and donate. Even in an increasingly secular world, churches and religious groups remain important concentrated hubs for civic participation.[4]

- **Community-level concern.** The Lewis Center highlights a "dollars up, donors down" reality—fewer people are giving even as some dollars rise—making everyday generosity more socially critical than ever.[5]

- **Global trends matter.** Worldwide surveys show dips in donating, volunteering, and helping strangers—reminding us why churches forming generous people matters, especially right now.[6, 7]

- **Science confirms it.** *Notre Dame's Science of Generosity* initiative has spent years studying this field, finding reliable benefits of generosity for happiness, health, and purpose—whether in children, adults, or seniors.[8]

WHY THIS MATTERS FOR MY CHILD (and yours)

I want my son to have a generous heart—not because I want him to be "nice," but because I want him to experience the joy that having an impact brings.

- ✦ Psychologically: Generosity trains attention off self and reduces anxiety by strengthening connection and meaning. Kids who practice giving taste the "helpers high" (dopamine/oxytocin effects) and learn agency—"I can make a difference."[9]

- ✦ Socially: Generosity builds bonding and bridging ties—friendships, community trust, and civic participation—exactly the social goods that are thinning in our cultural moment. Pew Research Group's civic work studies consistently show how important that is.[10]

- ✦ Spiritually: Generosity apprentices children to Jesus, freeing them from idolizing "more" and rooting their trust in God's provision. That's formation, not performance. And it gives them the ability to find joy whether times are lean or flush.

Here's the simple case these points reveal: *generosity is good for you, good for your family, and good for the world in which you live*—and it's how God grows your heart.

So we ask:

Lord, where would You have me be in my giving and in my living?

This question is not new. Followers of Jesus have been wrestling with it—and living out the answer—for centuries. The question now is, do *you* have the courage to wrestle with it?

RETHINKING TITHING

FINDING THE WAY AGAIN

When traveling with a compass and a map, it's startling how far off course you can get from the slightest misalignment. On a trail, if you keep your head down, focusing only on your footing and never look up to see the bigger picture, you can slowly drift of course until you're nowhere near the destination you intended. What starts as a one-degree shift can quickly become a detour of miles. Of course, it turns out this doesn't only apply to newbies. Professor Darran Wells, leader of the Outdoor Education and Recreation Program at Central Wyoming College —who literally wrote the book on "wilderness naviation" says, "In rolling terrain, thick forest, or weather that limits visibility, even the best navigators become disoriented."[11]

I learned that lesson the hard way while studying with Professor Wells in the mountains of the Wind River Range in Wyoming. I was following what I thought was the right heading, but without pausing to check the wider landscape, I wandered badly off track. Every landmark I thought I recognized turned out to be misleading. Wells saw my frustration and said, "Relax—merely being lost is not an emergency. Pause. Expand your view. Make the familiar stranger and look again."

We stopped. I lifted my eyes from the forest immediatly infront of me and gazed out at the ridges, valleys, and shadows in the distance. I let go of my mental map and reassessed my surroundings. And that's when I spotted the cairns—small stacks of stones that quietly mark the way in many backcountry wilderness areas or miles of petrified sand dunes. When you're aligned, they seem like obvious and unnecessary ornamentation. However, when you've strayed, they're lifelines. And that day, they brought me back on course.

The path of generosity and abundant living can pose much the same challenge. This is true regardless of how long you have been at the generosity game. You can be walking the "right" path—or at least think you are—you are sure your mental map is on point—yet slowly you drift because you haven't looked up in a while. Maybe you're doing what's legally correct or culturally expected, but your heart is no longer fixed on God. You're following the motions but missing the deeper motivation.

That's why giving isn't only about rules—it's about heart orientation—spiritual alignment. It's about looking up, seeing where the larger trail is headed, and making sure your steps align with the heart of God, not simply the habits that served you in the past.

MAKING THE FAMILIAR STRANGE

For many of us, the word *tithing* has been presented as a simple, fixed, biblical mandate: God commands 10%—no more, no less. But when we really dig into the biblical and historical context, the picture gets far more complicated—and far more interesting.

In the Old Testament, tithing looked very different from today:

- ✦ **Abraham** gave Melchizedek a tenth of the spoils from a battle (Gen. 14). It was a one-time, voluntary act, not a standing rule. Plus he was giving from resources gained on land that wasn't even his.

- ✦ **Jacob's vow** at Bethel (Gen. 28) revealed the early stirrings of faith. After waking from an encounter with God's presence in a dream, he pledged, well "If God will be with me… then I will give a tenth." This wasn't a binding command for all people; it was Jacob's way of saying, "I want my resources to bear witness to this relationship." His generosity was a tangible expression of trust in the God who had just promised to go with him—it was him leaning into the relationship.

- ✦ Under the **Mosaic Law**, tithes weren't only "for the church." They were a civic-religious tax that funded priests, Levites, public worship festivals, and care for widows, orphans, and immigrants (Num. 18; Deut. 14).

In the ancient world, generosity wasn't limited to tithing:

- ✦ Villages provided for one another through hospitality, gleaning laws, and communal responsibility (Lev. 19; Ruth 2).
- ✦ Wealthy patrons sponsored public works and religious life.
- ✦ Giving was relational, face-to-face, and woven into the fabric of community.

In the New Testament the model shifts into another gear. Jesus takes it further. He re-frames giving as part of devoting our whole selves to God (Matt. 22:37–38; Luke 14:33). It's certainly not about fulfilling a code—it's about proving who we serve:

> **"You cannot serve both God and mammon… where your treasure is, there your heart will be also."**
>
> **– Matthew 6:21, 24**

For Jesus, generosity is:

- ✦ **Heart-revealing** – a spiritual practice that shows who or what rules our life.

- ✦ **Needs-based** – giving what's required for the moment.

- ✦ **Mission-driven** – aimed at God's kingdom work.

Paul and the early church built on this spirit of giving. When they gathered money, it wasn't to maintain a temple tax system—it was to support their work and meet urgent needs. During famines and disasters, churches were called to send funds, food, and supplies to believers in other regions (Acts 11:27–30, 2 Cor. 8–9, Rom. 15: 25–27).

- Paul didn't say, "Make sure you've all tithed your 10%."

- He said, "Give what you can, so that there may be equality…your abundance supplying their need" (2 Cor. 8:13–14).

- The measure was the mission, not the percentage.

Modern giving is built in a different situation, and on a different system:

- ✦ Much of what tithing once covered is now funded through taxation—roads, schools, welfare.

- ✦ Land ownership, income-based currency, and property taxes create a completely different economic landscape.

- ✦ The biblical "tithe" doesn't map cleanly onto the way we live now.

When churches oversimplify this reality into, "God says give 10%," it's often done to make giving easy to remember and budget for—but it risks feelings of disconnection—or worse manipulation. People sense there's more to the story, and there is.

The truth is both more demanding and more freeing: In Christ, we're not bound to a fixed percentage. We're called to radical, cheerful, Spirit-led generosity—sometimes that's less than 10%, sometimes it's far more—but it's always meant to flow from love, not coercive compulsion.

If you make far more than you need, God also knows the power of what you can do. And trust me, there is joy in getting to distribute it and make an impact.

"ISN'T THIS JUST ABOUT MONEY?"

No! Money is only a part of Scripture's much wider vision of generosity. Time, talents, witness, and service are all important parts of it as well. The Lewis Center for Church Leadership reminds us that spiritual health is about whole-life stewardship, not merely monetary offerings. The reason this misunderstanding arises is because churches that narrate impact—changed lives, local needs met—tend to grow givers, because people give to mission, not machinery. By 'mission,' I mean the real stories of lives touched and communities changed; by 'machinery,' I mean budgets, utilities, paperwork, and institutional upkeep. The machinery is necessary, but it's the mission that inspires the heart to give.

Generosity is not simply a virtue for the naturally warm-hearted or the deeply religious. It is part of our design as human beings, woven into us by the Creator who made us in His image. When we give—our time, our skills, our resources—we participate in God's ongoing work of creation and redemption.

REORIENTING OUR GENEROSITY COMPASS

So how do we reorient our giving and living?

Through intentional reflection and response. That's why I've prepared this devotional built around a simple, life-shaping question, which I was once encouraged to pray myself:

Lord, where would You have me be in my giving and in my living?

To answer that question honestly, you may have to let go of what's familiar—because that's what allows God to lead us into new patterns. Sometimes we've been giving with strings attached, directing our resources toward what we prefer, rather than what God desires. But true generosity is not about fulfilling our own vision—it's about yielding entirely to God's.

This isn't about guilt or hitting a number—it's about taking the journey with God, asking Him to guide your generosity, and discovering the joy of participating in God's generosity toward the world.

A LEGACY OF TRUSTWORTHY GENEROSITY

John Wesley, the founder of the Anglican evangelical revival we now call the Methodist movement, believed life is a precious gift from God—and what we do with that gift matters. In his writings and speeches he often argued that if the Kingdom of God is to reach every corner of creation, then spiritual devotion must be paired with practical action—and that includes the way we handle our money.

Wesley summed it up in three simple rules:

1. **Earn all you can** — without harming your health, your integrity, or others.

2. **Save all you can** — by living simply, not hoarding, so that you are free to give your life away and maximize your impact.

3. **Give all you can** — pouring resources into God's work in the world.

Wesley didn't merely preach this—he practiced it. In 1731, he began limiting his expenses to free up more to give to the poor. That first year he made 30 pounds, lived on 28, and gave away 2. The next year he made 60 pounds, still lived on 28, and gave away 32. Later, when he earned 120 pounds, he still lived on 28 and gave away 92.

He was famously frugal. In an age when a man in his highly respected position was expected to own an expensive white powdered wig, he bought a second-hand one instead—choosing what was adequate so he could maximize what he gave.

INTEGRITY THAT EARNS TRUST

This call to handle resources faithfully isn't unique to Wesley. For the first three centuries of the Christian era, believers were known for their integrity with money.

Take the story of Sarapammon, a pagan Olympic champion in the third century. He wrote to his mother from Antioch to tell her he was sending **two talents**—the equivalent of forty years' wages for a laborer. He entrusted this fortune to a man named Sotas, "the Christian."

Think about that. At a time when Christianity was illegal, Sarapammon still chose a Christian to deliver his life savings—because believers had a reputation for honesty and trustworthiness. Generosity had shaped their character, and character had built their reputation.

DIRECTING RESOURCES TOWARD LIFE

Generosity isn't only about the personal virtue of the giver—it's about what those resources make possible.

Pastor Johnny Ray Youngblood, of Saint Paul's Community Church in Brooklyn, ministered in one of the poorest, most crime-ridden neighborhoods in America. His church transformed brothels into apartments, launched job training, started AA groups, and offered business classes for youth.

Part of his process in making all this happen was asking for donations from those they served. When asked why he would do such a thing, Youngblood replied: "The problem in Brooklyn wasn't a lack of money. It was what people were doing with their money that was killing them."

He knew the deep truth of what Jesus, and later Wesley, taught:

what we do with our money shapes who we become, and it shapes the community around us.

BRINGING IT HOME

The New Testament calls us to be abundantly—even outrageously—generous. Wesley would say, *"Give all YOU can."* That means we don't measure ourselves by someone else's ability or calling. We measure ourselves by how we respond to what God is asking of us personally.

That's the heart of this devotional: not to get you to hit a certain number, but to get you to courageously step out and ask:

Lord, where would You have me be
in *my* giving and in *my* living?

And then to have the courage to stay with the question until an answer comes.

DAILY DEVOTIONALS WEEK 1

LEAVING THE TRAILHEAD

DAY 1 — Fear on the Trail

Numbers 13:25–28

On certain trails, the most intimidating thing isn't the climb itself—it's the first glimpse of it. You round a corner and there it is: switchbacks stacked into the clouds, a ridge so narrow you can see the drop on both sides. Every instinct tells you to turn back. That's exactly what happened to the Israelites. They'd scouted the land God promised—lush valleys, rich soil, fruit so heavy it took two men to carry it. But they'd also seen fortified cities and giants. "It's good," they admitted, "but it's too risky."

Fear works the same way with generosity. The news headlines shout about layoffs, inflation, and uncertainty. Budgets feel tight. And somewhere inside, a voice whispers, "Not now. Play it safe." Fear magnifies the obstacles and shrinks the promise. But God is the Owner—of the trail, the land, and the harvest. We're the sowers, planting trust step by step. The path isn't always easy, but it's His path. And the One who calls us forward will guide our feet where they need to go.

Reflection: Where is fear keeping you at the trailhead instead of stepping into God's promises?

DAY 2 — The Unexpected Detour

Exodus 3:1–4

On the best hikes, you sometimes find yourself sidetracked by unexpected beauty—a side path to a hidden waterfall, a wildflower meadow in full bloom. Moses wasn't looking for a mission that day in the wilderness; he was looking after sheep. But when he saw a bush burning without being burnt up, he stopped. He turned aside. And in that pause, God called his name.

Spirit-led generosity often starts with the same kind of holy interruption. You're on your normal path—paying bills, checking emails—when God nudges you to give, help, or invest in something you hadn't planned for. Andy Stanley once asked, *"If your money knew about God and knew your passions, where would it ask you to put it to work?"* Sometimes the only way to answer that question is to step off the main trail and see where God is leading.

God's abundance fills the world around us long before we are aware of it. Turning aside to notice is how we learn to sow from that abundance. The trail is never simply about the miles—it's about the moments you would have missed if you hadn't stopped to look.

Reflection: When has God used an unexpected moment to shift your direction toward generosity with your time, your money, your knowledge, your resources, or your talents?

DAY 3 — Carrying Doubt and Still Climbing

Exodus 4:10–13

Halfway up the mountain is where most hikers think about turning back. The adrenaline from the trailhead is gone, the summit still hidden in the clouds. The pack begins to come heavy with all the extra things you thought you needed. Moses had his halfway moment too. God had called him, equipped him, and given him a vision—and still Moses said, "I'm not eloquent… I can't do this… send someone else." The expectations he carried for himself were getting in the way of the journey.

Generosity can be affected the same way. You start with a stirring in your heart, but then the realities close in: bills, tuition, medical costs, streaming subscriptions, concert tickets, new home decor, a boat. Adam Hamilton calls it "credit-itis"—that cultural condition where debt and obligations crowd out joy. But just like on the trail, there's a way forward. Sometimes you adjust the straps, lighten the load, and take one more step.

A friend of mine once told me she started her generosity journey unsure if she could give at all. Then she began trimming her spending in small, intentional ways—a subscription here, a habit there. She called it "cutting weight from the pack." And by the time she reached her Commitment Sunday, she was giving more than she ever thought possible, and with more joy than she imagined.

Reflection: What "pack weight" could you cut in order to grow your potential for Spirit-led generosity?

DAY 4 — Stars Above the Campsite

Genesis 15:1, 3, 5–6

On long hikes, there's a special kind of stillness after the campfire dies down. You step out from the tent, tilt your head back, and see a sky crowded with stars. Stars so thick they don't look like connect the dots, but you swear you can see detailed faces of the heroes and animals for which the constellations were named. That's the moment God gave to Abram. He had followed God's call into unknown country, but now his hands were empty—no child, no heir. His hope was running out. So God took him outside and said, "Count the stars, if you can… so shall your descendants be."

Generosity is about more than meeting the needs of the present —it's about joining God in a story that stretches beyond us to more than we can imagine. The gifts we sow today will grow into moments we may never see: a child learning to pray, a neighbor finding Christ, a hungry family fed. When we give, we're trusting in the stars—investing in promises that are bigger than what we can see. God doesn't expect us to produce the harvest—only to keep sowing, cultivating, and tending in trust.

Reflection: Which promises of God are you investing in that will still shine long after you're gone?

DAY 5 — Setting the Pack in Order

Joshua 3:5

The Jordan River shimmered just up ahead. On the far side lay the Promised Land—but the river beform them was wide and rushing. The people didn't know how they'd cross the swiftly moving waters. And Joshua didn't give them a plan. But he gave them a command: "Sanctify yourselves." In other words, prepare your hearts and minds for what's next. God was about to move, and they needed to be ready. It was a call to, "Be worthy of where God is leading us."

Anyone who has spent time in the wilderness knows that preparation is part of the adventure. Before a big climb or trek, you check your gear. Not every tool belongs on every journey. If you're climbing Mt. Everest, you don't strap a whitewater raft to your back. You carry only what's needed—and you make sure you know how to use it. The right preparation can be the difference in finishing strong and being forced to turn back.

In the same way, God often asks us to prepare before the next part of our faith journey. But this preparation goes deeper than packing the correct supplies. It's about clearing clutter from our lives, aligning our desires with His, and cultivating contentment. It's about learning to live as trustees of God's abundance—so that when God says, "Go," we're light enough and prepared enough to move with Him.

Reflection: What clutter—financial, spiritual, or emotional—needs to come out of your pack before the next part of the journey?

SMALL GROUP GUIDE - WEEK 1

Leaving the Trailhead (Days 1–5)

Confronting fear, answering the call, preparing your pack.

Opening Check-In

When have you stood at the edge of a big decision, unsure if you could take the first step? What helped you move forward?

Scripture Reading

Numbers 13:27–28, Exodus 3–4; Luke 5:1–11

Insight & Reflection

Starting the trail is thrilling and intimidating. The disciples, Moses, and Joshua all faced their own "trailhead moments." Fear is loud at the beginning—it tells you you're not enough, you're not ready. But God's call doesn't wait for your confidence, it invites your trust.

Discussion Questions

1. What kinds of "giants" or challenges feel most intimidating right now—in life, faith, or generosity?

2. How do you tell the difference between the voice of fear and the voice of God?

3. What's in your "pack" right now? Are there fears or burdens you need to leave behind before moving forward?

Group Practice

Invite each person to name one fear or obstacle they want to entrust to God this week. Pray over them, asking for courage to take the first step.

Closing Prayer

Lord of Love,
You call us to follow You into places unknown.
Grant us the courage to take the first step, even when fear attempts to hold us back.
Lighten our load of worry and self-doubt.
Fill our hearts with trust in Your voice and our minds with the vision of where You're leading.
Amen

DAILY DEVOTIONALS WEEK 2

TRUSTING GOD'S PACE

DAY 1 — Standing Still at the Crossing

2 Chronicles 20:13–15, 17

There are moments on the trail when the river is running high and fast, and the safest thing you can do is… nothing. Rushing in without thought can sweep you off your feet, ruin your gear, or send you miles downstream from where you meant to land. If you cross in the wrong place, it might cost you precious daylight to get back—or force you to take the risk again. Worse, if your gear gets soaked and the sun goes down before you can dry out, you could find yourself in a life-threatening situation. That's why experienced hikers stop first—they study the current, scan for the shallows, and decide if today is even the right day to cross. Some crossings aren't won by a quick pace; they're won by patience.

When King Jehoshaphat faced a vast enemy, God's message was the same: "Take your position, stand still, and see the victory of the Lord." We live in a culture that tells us to always push harder—solve the problem, hustle, do more. But generosity sometimes begins with stillness: pausing to listen, letting the Spirit set the pace. It's handing control of the map back to God. When we stop scrambling to manage every outcome, we find the courage to give without the need to see how it all works out.

Reflection: Where in your financial life is God inviting you to pause, listen, and trust before you move? How about in your schedule?

DAY 2 — More Than the Map Shows

Ephesians 3:20–21

Trail maps are helpful tools. They can outline ridges, warn of cliffs that are impassable without gear, mark water sources, and point to high meadows perfect for camping. But they can't capture everything—the breathtaking view around the bend, the wildflowers tucked in the shade, the hidden waterfall just out of sight. Paul reminds us that God works the same way: "far more than all we can ask or imagine."

I once knew a woman named Sally who loved her church family and wanted to participate financially in the ministries of the church, but believed she had nothing significant to give. Her husband, not a churchgoer, handled the family finances. Still, she prayed. On Commitment Sunday, he surprised her—not only showing up, but writing a gift far larger than anything she had dared to imagine. He'd seen what the church meant to her and the impact it had through its partnerships with Scouts, philanthropic clubs, and missions. His heart was moved, and doors for the ministries she cherished opened wider than she ever thought possible.

Generosity isn't about your capacity—it's about God's. Living generously with your time, talents, and resources means not just planning for the possible, but trusting God with the impossible. So remember the trail belongs to Him. Keep walking—there's always more than the map shows.

Reflection: Where might God be preparing something bigger than you're asking for? Are you bold enough to pray for it and commit it to Him, saying, "Thy will be done"?

DAY 3 — Anchored on the Ridge

Ephesians 3:14–19

Ridge walking—traversing across a balance beam-esque rocky outcroping at the top of a mountain—is one of my favorite activities. It can be absolutely beautiful. It offers endless, breathtaking views in every direction, but it's also exposed. Winds can push you off balance, clouds can hide the trail. Those that hike such lines must know how to anchor themselves—sometimes literally—before taking the next step.

I once scrambled along such a ridge with my friend John. It was an ancient line that looked like a dragon's spine fossilized in the sunshine and worn with time. Much of the rock was brittle, and broke away under any carelessly placed step. Every footing had to be tested. All along the way, great stone spires rose from the ridge—towers of rock anchored deep into the earth, immovable no matter how the wind roared or the rain pounded against them. Between them, the ridge narrowed to merely enough space for a single careful step, reminding us that our safety depended on keeping to what was firmly grounded.

Out upon the brittle ridgeline, your life depends on what you anchor to. In faith, it's no different—which is why Paul's prayer for the Ephesians was that they would be "rooted and grounded in love." In the same way, the giving of our time and resources must be anchored not in fear or pressure, but in the steadfast nature of God's love. Without that anchor, we reach for footholds that crumble beneath us—a certain savings number, a bigger house, the next promotion. God's love received first is the solid bedrock upon which all else rest. Those other things are like loose rock that shifts and crumbles under foot.

Generosity isn't measured by the amount, but by the heart that anchors it. When we commit a portion of our time, our income, or our abilities to God, we set our feet against something that will not move, trusting the One who knows the ridge and the view beyond it.

Reflection: What "false anchors" do you find yourself reaching for when life feels uncertain? How can you reset your feet upon the solid rock?

DAY 4 — Love that Gives First

John 3:16–17

On a long trek, every ounce in your pack matters. Comforts from home are often left behind to save weight. But as the days pass and your pack grows lighter, you start wishing you'd slipped in something extra.

One afternoon, halfway through a month long backpacking excursion a group I was with sat together resting our legs, trading stories of home and the little things we missed most—warm bread fresh out of the oven, the taste of an espresso, Mom's famous ratatouille, Chicken Tikka Masala at the Indian buffett… greasy French fries, juicy hamburgers, a soft-serve ice cream cone so runny the sprinkles cascade off the peak and must be licked off your hand. We laughed, sighed, and let our minds wander to the comforts we'd left behind. Then, without a word, a friend reached into her pack and pulled out a chocolate bar—a small treasure she'd carried meant for a private moment by herself.

She could have kept it hidden, but love moves first. She broke it into pieces and passed them around. Each little bit wasn't much for each of us, but the sweetness was more than flavor—it was the joy of sharing, the warmth of the memory, the delight of a gift freely given. And as a result she gained a memory, a moment she could cherish forever. Long after the chocolate was gone, what stayed with us was the sweetness of belonging—that sacred sense that we were in it together, sharing more than food, sharing life.

Love moves first. "For God so loved the world that He gave…" Love doesn't wait for the perfect moment or the guarantee of return. It sees the need, feels the longing, and moves toward it. On the trail, sharing what you have lightens both your pack and someone else's burden. In life, giving from love lightens your spirit and brings hope to others.

We don't give because we must. We give because the power of love, resides in our act of giving it away.

Reflection: Who is God bringing to mind right now that needs the kind of love that gives first?

DAY 5 — Gratitude at Base Camp

2 Corinthians 9:11–12

Base camp. It's where climbers prepare for the summit—checking supplies, sharing resources, and encouraging one another. It's a place where strength is pooled for the sake of the journey ahead. Gratitude works the same way in the journey of generosity and abundant living. Paul says our giving "overflows with many thanksgivings to God."

One of my most memorable "base camps" was a small church outside Wasilla, Alaska. It served as our home for a week of construction and landscaping projects during a mission trip. In the mornings, the fellowship hall smelled faintly of coffee, evergreens, and fresh-cut lumber from the nearby job sites. Backpacks and tool bags leaned against the walls. Boots dried by the door. Laughter and snippets of story drifted over the hum of a space heater. It was the kind of place where people gathered not because they had to, but because they wanted to be there.

Our team had come because of what God had done in our lives —grateful for His grace and eager to serve. The congregation, though unable to join us much on the work site, wanted to give something in return. They decided to host a potluck. I didn't know what to expect, but what they brought stunned me: fresh-caught salmon, moose noodle casserole, elk sliders, vegetable & bear stew, caribou sausage, deviled eggs from local farms, greenhouse greens still crisp from the morning harvest. These were the fruits of their labor, gathered from the land and waters that sustained them. They gave the best they had, and they gave it gladly.

That night, gratitude flowed in both directions. We were blessed to receive their generosity; they were blessed to give from what God had provided. In that exchange, we experienced the deep truth of Paul's words—that true giving is never one-way. Gratitude grows in both the giver and the receiver, and it overflows into joy, worship, and deeper relationships.

Reflection: Where have you seen gratitude flow both ways—in your giving and your receiving? How can you step into that kind of mutual blessing this week?

SMALL GROUP GUIDE - WEEK 2

Trusting God's Pace (Days 6–10)

Stillness, surprise provision, and gratitude as fuel

Opening Check-In

What's something in your life you had to wait for? What did you discover in the waiting?

Scripture Reading

Genesis 15, Joshua 3, 2 Chronicles 20, Matthew 6:25–34

Insight & Reflection

On the trail, speed isn't everything—endurance is. The Israelites at the Jordan had to "stand still and see" before stepping forward. Generosity is the same: it flows best when we match God's pace, noticing His provision along the way. One of the ways we can do that is through actively stating our gratitude for the things we witness or experience.

Discussion Questions

1. What does "standing still" look like for you spiritually?

2. How does gratitude help you stay steady when you feel restless and uncertain?

3. Can you recall a time when God provided for you in a surprising way?

Group Practice

Have each member of the group share one thing they're grateful for this week. Then invite people to use it as the first deposit into their gratitude tank—a cup or jar they can place notes into of things they are grateful for each day. Have them accumulate these and then read them before the following week begins as encouragement for the week ahead. May this gratitude be "fuel" for the adventure that lies before them.

Closing Prayer

God of perfect timing,
Slow our racing thoughts and steady our hurried steps.
Help us match Your pace so that we don't miss Your provision along the way.
Teach us to walk with open eyes, grateful hearts, and patient trust in what You are doing.
Put another way, Lord, Thy will be done.
Amen

DAILY DEVOTIONALS WEEK 3

COURAGEOUS CLIMBS

DAY 1 — Joy that Overflows

2 Corinthians 8:1–2

The value of some gifts is immeasurably more than their price tag suggests.

Spending time in the wilderness teaches you to a radical degree the difference between what you desire and what you truly need. Days away from stores, screens, and conveniences strip life down to the essentials. Most backpackers take this seriously, but some take it to the extreme. They're called ultralighters—for them, every ounce matters, to the point of cutting toothbrush handles in half, leaving behind any extra or backup items, trimming their dishwashing sponge, and even refusing to take along a good book.

I'm not an ultralighter. I'm in the camp that believes your backpack should be ever so slightly too heavy. Not overloaded, but heavy enough to carry a few "unnecessary" things on purpose—something that brings an extra dose of joy, beauty, or connection to your adventure.

That's why I carry a small deck of cards and a bag of locally roasted coffee. Yes, they make my pack a little heavier, but that's a deliberate trade-off I'm willing to make. The moments that these items create—laughter around a game, the smell of coffee drifting through camp, a warm cup shared with a friend—are worth every ounce.

Generosity works the same way. We can strip our lives down to what's strictly "necessary," or we can choose to carry something extra for the sake of others. Jesus calls us to live with enough margin that we can give freely. Sometimes the thing you give may seem small—even unnecessary—but when it's offered with love, it becomes the most meaningful thing in the pack.

Years ago, I was in India helping a boy named Aarav with his English. We practiced words and phrases, laughed at our mistakes, and slowly found our rhythm. When our lessons ended, he pulled something out of his pocket and placed it in my hand—a small black plastic rosary. It couldn't have cost much, but he purchased it with his own money and he was immensely proud of it.

I knew Aarav's family situation and what that money could have meant for him. But I did not protest the gift. Instead, I allowed the shock and delight—at both the kindness and the meaning behind the gift—to become fully visible on my face. While it was something I never would have bought for myself. Aarav bought it with what little he had, and the heart that accompanied it made that cheap plastic rosary priceless. To this day, it remains one of my most cherished possessions.

Jesus says, "Give, and it will be given to you… for with the measure you use it will be measured back to you." Aarav didn't give from abundance—he gave from love. And that small token of appreciation was made priceless because it carried the giver's heart. In receiving it, I learned in a fresh way that generosity blesses both the giver and the receiver in ways no price tag can measure. And I hope, and trust, that the time I donated to tutoring him is cherished the much the same way.

Reflection: What's something small you could give this week that would carry great meaning for someone else?

DAY 2 — First to the Lord

2 Corinthians 8:3–5

Paul says the Macedonian believers gave "first to the Lord" and then to others, even beyond their means. They weren't just generous; they understood that caring for the community ultimately safeguarded them, too. In God's economy, the blessing of one becomes the blessing of all.

Years ago, my friend Crystal went on an expedition of another type. She studied abroad in Australia. There she spent her days working in a hospital and serving in a local church. Just before she was set to return home, her grandfather passed away unexpectedly. Crystal longed to be at his funeral, but she hadn't yet saved enough money for the $688 ticket home. At that point, she had only $40 left in her wallet.

One night at church, a need was shared about a remote community devastated by a natural disaster. They had no clean drinking water and little access to basic resources. As the offering plate was passed, the pastor invited everyone to pray: "Ask God what He is calling you to give."

Crystal whispered a prayer and reached for a $20 bill. But in that moment, she sensed God saying, "I want it all." She hesitated, proud of her step of faith, but again heard the same whisper: "I want it all." Those twenty-dollar bills were everything she had left—her only hope of making it back home for the funeral. Still, she responded in faith, placed the money in the plate, and prayed, "Lord, I trust You."

That night she dreamed of opening a small ornate box filled with colorful scraps of paper.

The next day at work, her coworkers—who knew she was grieving her grandfather but didn't know about her financial need—surprised her. They handed her a small ornate wooden box. Inside were handwritten notes of encouragement on brightly colored scraps of paper, and tucked between them were Australian bills of various amounts. For those who don't know, Australian currency comes in different colors by denomination —it was a rainbow of bills.

When she counted the total, it was the exact amount she needed for her flight home: $688.

First-fruits giving is about setting up the whole team for success. On the trail, you don't wait to share what's left at the bottom of your pack—you share first, trusting that everyone will have enough to finish the journey. In the same way, giving first is both an act of faith and a kind of spiritual wisdom. It says, "I trust the Owner of the trail to supply what I'll need for the rest of the journey." In God's Kingdom, a community where needs are met up front is the strongest safety net you'll ever know.

Of course, the roles we play in that community shift, but in a healthy, God-shaped community, giving and receiving are not opposites but part the rhythm of God's love. When we learn to receive without shame, and to give without fear we experience the abundance that God desires for us.

Reflection: What would it look like for *you* to give your "first fruits" to God?

DAY 3 — Making God Real on the Trail

1 Corinthians 10:31 – 11:1

On long-distance trails, there's a special breed of kindness called *trail magic*. It comes from *trail angels*—people who go out of their way to help hikers. Sometimes it's a cooler of cold drinks left at a dusty trailhead, a ride into town, or a home-cooked meal in a stranger's kitchen. You can't earn it, and you usually can't repay it. You simply have to receive it with amazement and gratitude that someone who saw your need and quietly stepped in.

That's how God often works—through people whose love shows up at just the right moment. I think of a young couple in a church I served who had been saving for years to remodel their home. When a ministry need arose, they prayed and sensed God asking them to give that money instead. Their house stayed the same, but their hearts didn't. Like trail angels, the power of their gift now blesses people who may never know their names but will certainly feel the ripple of their generosity in the new programs and renovated spaces their gift made possible.

Following Jesus means leaving a trail of God's love behind you —acts of kindness and generosity that make the presence of God real to weary travelers. You never know whose strength might be renewed because of it.

Paul calls us to "do everything to the glory of God... so that many may be saved." That "everything" includes our generous giving so that God may be made real to all those we meet.

Reflection: When people look at how you use your time, energy, and resources, do they see the trail magic of God's love?

DAY 4 — Trust to the Uttermost

Mark 10:21–27

On the river, trust is everything. I remember paddling with friends when we came up on a section of rapids we hadn't run before. The roar grew louder as we approached—we knew we had to pull over. We dragged our kayaks onto the bank, climbed the ridge, and walked downstream to scout things out.

Below us churned a Class IV rapid – big, technical water that demands precise maneuvers, split-second timing, and the humility to know it can flip you fast and hold you down. We had a decision to make: run it, or portage around. The current would not let us hop out halfway through. Trusting ourselves meant committing all the way.

Jesus said something similar about wealth. He warned that the danger isn't about having resources; it's depending on them as if they can carry you safely through life's rapids. At some point, every disciple has to decide: will I trust the current of God's provision, or will I cling to the illusion of control?

I once knew a couple, the Johansons, who had faced their own rapid. They had pledged a generous gift to the church—and then their investments crashed. They could have pulled back. But instead, they said, *"Because of what God has done for us... we will trust."* And they gave anyway, unsure how the rest of the year would unfold.

Three months later, an unexpected bonus arrived—almost to the dollar of their pledge. What had felt like a reckless step became a powerful reminder that God already knew what lay downstream. Needless to say, the timing stunned them.

Returns like this won't always come in the same way—but the God who sees the whole trail knows what's ahead and what's on the way.

Trusting to the uttermost doesn't always mean the outcome looks neat or financial provision arrives right away or in your way. Sometimes it means portaging around an obstacle or two. Sometimes it means running the rapid. Either way, the decision isn't about control—it's about faith in the One who owns the river, sees the course, and knows what's waiting beyond the spray.

Reflection: What "rapids" or challenges in your life require you to scout ahead with prayer and trust?

DAY 5 — The Strength in the Stillness

Isaiah 40:29–31

Isaiah reminds us that those who *"wait for the Lord"* will renew their strength, run without weariness, and walk without fainting. On a long climb, the wisest hikers know the value of a good rest stop—moments to shed the pack, breathe deeply, and take in their surroundings.

If the summit is the only thing that matters, we turn what is meant to be a journey into merely a legalistic checkbox, and we miss life in the forest. Hiking through the mountains isn't simply about getting to the other side—it's about noticing life along the way. When you pause to sit, the forest comes alive around you. Birds flutter in, insects buzz by, and woodland creatures begin to scurry about, no longer so shy. The summit view is grand, but it's not where you'll see the beauty of life in motion. The stillness along the way holds its own reward.

Sometimes we think rest is wasted time, but rest is actually where strength is built and joy is renewed. It's in these quiet spaces that God reshapes our hearts, recharges our spirits, and realigns our priorities.

Ben learned this while taking evening walks with his dog, Callie. Each night, he'd circle the church and pray a simple prayer: *Lord, what would You have me do for You?* One evening, he paused on a bench. In the stillness, life moved around him—a runner passed, neighbors chatted, children biked through the lot, someone waited in the shade for the bus, and a woman prayed by the memorial pond.

He remained until the sun began to set, and in that moment, Ben felt God whisper, *Help Me reach them.* He realized that increased generosity could mean more events, more staff, and more opportunities to connect with people just like these. By the time Commitment Sunday rolled around Ben's planned gift doubled—not from impulse, but from the deep clarity that stillness had given him. He also signed up to serve on the evangelism committee, eager to match his giving with hands-on ministry.

Rest and generosity go hand in hand. Both require humility—letting go of control, trusting God's sufficiency, and opening our lives to others. When we rest, we're reminded that all we have is His to use—not ours to clutch.

Reflection: Where can you carve out a moment of stillness this week—not just to renew your strength, but to delight in the journey—and open your heart to the whispers of God?

SMALL GROUP GUIDE - WEEK 3

Courageous Climbs

Sacrificial giving, first fruits, anchored trust

Opening Check-In

When have you taken a leap of faith that cost you something—but was worth it?

Scripture Reading

2 Corinthians 8:9, Mark 12:38–44, Proverbs 3:9–10

Insight & Reflection

Every trail has steep climbs. Climbs require strength, commitment, and trust in the path. In the same way, giving from the "first fruits" isn't about having excess; it's about putting our priorities in order and our trust in God's supply before we see the summmit.

Discussion Questions

1. What's the difference between giving from overflow and giving sacrificially?

2. How do you anchor your trust in God when resources feel tight?

3. What motivates you more—obligation or vision?

Group Practice

Invite the group to write one new way or place they could be generous this week—time, attention, or resources—and pray for courage to act on it.

Closing Prayer — Responsive Blessing

Leader: For the courage to take the next step…
Group: We give thanks.

Leader: For the strength to give first the faith to trust, and the grace to release what we hold…
Group: We give thanks.

Leader: May our courage not stop with us—but inspire others to climb with faith.
Group: Amen.

DAILY DEVOTIONALS WEEK 4

THE SUMMIT

DAY 1 — Waiting with Eyes Open

Psalm 130:5–7

Some hikes teach you that patience pays in ways the map can't predict. When I lived in Kauai, I often hiked to the overlook above the Nāpali Coast—a view so breathtaking it could be mistaken for a painting. But many days, the scene would be swallowed in thick clouds. Tourists would arrive, see nothing but mist, and groan in disappointment. I'd tell them, *"Wait fifteen minutes—the wind will shift."* Some stayed. Some left. And it never failed—the ones who stayed were rewarded when the clouds lifted, revealing cliffs and ocean in their full splendor. The ones who left missed it entirely.

The psalmist writes, *"I wait for the Lord, my soul waits, and in His word I hope."* That's not a passive kind of waiting; it's an expectant one—the kind that believes the view will open because it trusts in the one behind it.

Sometimes in church life—let's be honest, often—growth and change take longer than we'd like. *I gave the gift, I'm being a good steward... so why isn't anything happening yet?* But giving doesn't mean God now operates on our timeline. The prayer is still *"Thy will be done,"* not *"My schedule be kept."*

On the generosity trail, waiting with eyes open means holding to your commitment even when the "view" isn't clear yet—when you can't see how your gift is being used, when the impact feels hidden in the mist of God's mystery. Some give up too soon, leaving before the moment God was preparing comes into view.

At worst their "This isn't going to work" mentality becomes a self-fulfilling prophecy that undermines the ministry and tears it apart. But most often it simply takes a little longer. Those who stay. Those who trust God's timing. One day they are rewarded, with getting to see and experience the breathtaking evidence of His provision and the impact of their faith.

In ministry, the balance between transparency and privacy sometimes means the work God is doing stays veiled for a season. It's like He's assembling a masterpiece under cover. The anticipation can be hard—but if you'll wait, the unveiling is worth it.

Reflection: Are you willing to wait long enough for the view that God has been preparing for you all along to emerge?

DAY 2 — The Sound of Stillness

Psalm 46:10

On the trail, there's a stillness you can't find anywhere else. It is often into that place that some of my grandest ideas and clearest insights arrive. I can spend months wrestling with a problem in the office, pushing hard for a solution, but no matter how much I strain, the answer won't come. Then I'll step onto a hiking trail, be halfway into a 5 mile loop, immersed in the still hum of nature—the wind through the pines, the quaking of the aspens, a creek murmuring below—and without warning, the key insight I've been longing for—drops into place. Something about the stillness opens a door my striving never could.

This devotional journey has been filled with one question: ***Lord, where would You have me be in my giving and in my living?***

We've asked this question not to see if we are meeting some external standard, but to reveal an answer to the question: ***Is my heart growing in maturity as a disciple?*** It's a simple question, but it can feel daunting to ask. Part of us fears the answer—after all, Jesus once told a man, "One thing you lack: go, sell all you have, and follow Me." But we worry, *What if God says that to me?* And right when we work up the courage to finally ask such a question, life interrupts with a thousand little distractions.

Oftentimes—once we build up the courage to open our heart to God—what we need most is a clear space where God can be heard without the static of modern life.

People find such space in many ways. My friend Paul finds it on the trail, Bill finds it on his bike, Kristi finds it while doing needlepoint. One man I know found that space in the shower. It became his private chapel—a place where no emails pinged, no to-do lists pressed in, no kids interrupted with questions. There, in the steam and quiet, he prayed the same question again and again: ***Lord, I pray thy will be done. Where would You have me be in my giving and in my living?***

Over time, that question reshaped his heart. At first, he held it with anxiety—measuring himself against an invisible yardstick marked with paycheck percentages and hours volunteered. But eventually, his concern over the exact amount he gave faded, replaced by the joy of simply being part of a church family making a real impact in the world.

On the generosity trail, the best navigation happens when we stop to listen. Stillness isn't wasted time; it's where our hearts align with God's will, our fear is replaced with trust, and the way forward becomes clear.

Reflection: Where can you make space for stillness so generosity flows from listening and relationship, not only logic?

DAY 3 — Gratitude that Overflows

2 Corinthians 9:11–13

Basecamps aren't only for rest—they're for sharing stories and gratitude, too. They're the place where the day's sweat turns into tales of glory and grace, where blisters and bruises become badges of honor, and where you remember you didn't get here alone. You think of the stranger who loaned you her knife, the teammate who refilled your water when your energy was sapped, the weather that held off just long enough for you to make it in. Around the basecamp fire, you recall these things, and in them, you find the beautiful generosity of the day.

My great teacher in this art of campfire gratitude was my Aunt Tammy. She taught me how to tell stories around a campfire and sprinkle in questions that held a deeper purpose. She never did the traditional "highs and lows" thing. Instead, she'd ask: *What was the coolest thing you experienced today? The most courageous thing you saw today? The thing you're most grateful for?* Those campfires grounded me. They became the launchpad for the next day's adventure—and, eventually, for stepping back into the school year after a summer of exploration.

My Aunt Tammy and Uncle Scott's generosity—of time, wisdom, and love—created memories that I still draw from today. Their gift overwhelms me with gratitude and reminds me of Paul's words: generosity "produces thanksgiving to God."

My friend Judy experienced that same kind of generosity through her church family. Her son Kevin has special needs, and she once told me, "It's easy to feel isolated when your child is different. I can't imagine what life would have been like if I didn't have my church family for support. Kevin has grown up here since he was two, and in every stage of life there's been someone ready with a hug, a smile, or a kind word at exactly the right time."

When Kevin's father died a few years back, that same network of love became Judy's anchor.

For Judy, the gratitude and generosity she's found in her church family is a launching pad—one she wants others to experience too. She doesn't give out of duty or obligation; she gives out of deep thankfulness for the people who have walked with she and Kevin every step of the way. Gratitude shifted her giving from "*I have to*" into "*I get to.*" It's like the warmth of stories and reflection around the campfire at day's end—where stories are shared, courage is kindled, and strength for the next leg of the journey is found. Pass that kind of warmth along, and it can light the way for more people than you ever imagined., it can warm so many more than you can imagined.

Reflection: How has God—or God's people—carried you through a season when you couldn't carry yourself?

DAY 4

Mark 2:3–5

Four friends carried a paralyzed man to Jesus. When the door was blocked, they climbed the roof, dug through, and lowered him down. Each had a corner of the mat—no one carried the whole weight, but together they brought him to the Healer.

I was once part of a cave rescue that made me look at this lesson in a whole new way. We were carrying a man strapped into a stretcher through narrow passages and over uneven rock. The air was damp, our backs ached, and every step mattered. One member of our team wasn't on stretcher duty. Instead, she walked ahead, shining her light on each foothold and calling out where we needed to step.

Honestly? At first, it was a little annoying. She kept asking, "Is there anything more I can do?" We were all tired, and her role wasn't as physically strenuous as ours. But as the hours wore on, our feet grew less steady and our focus less clear. Someone wobbled a bit. And that's when she asked again, "Is there anything else I can do? Am I doing enough?"

That's when one of the stretcher team members turned to her and said, "Are we all safe?" She nodded. "Then it's enough. The weight is heavy, but we've got it. What we need is for you to keep us safe. We need you right where you are."

In that moment, something seemed to click for her—she realized what we all already knew. Without her voice guiding us, we could have tripped, stumbled, and dropped the stretcher in a dangerous spot. She was our eyes. She was our pathfinder. And her job was vital.

Generosity works much the same way. Your part may not look like someone else's, but it matters. You may not be called to give as much. You may not be called to a highly visible position. You may end up counting the offering in an unseen room somewhere. But that job is no less vitally importnat to the process of checks and balances—and therefore the integrity of the church.

Sometimes carrying your corner of the mat means giving direction, holding the light, organizing the team, packing the bags, or steadying someone else's load. Other times it's about giving financially or simply showing up. Often, it's a mix of things. Whatever it is that God has called you to in this moment—trust that it's enough.

Reflection: What does it look like for you to faithfully carry your corner in this season?

DAY 5 — Hearts on Fire at the Summit

Luke 24:32

Reaching the summit after days on the trail is about more than a view. It's a flood of memory: every step, every challenge, every moment you thought you couldn't go on. You stand there, lungs burning, look out over the horizon, and realize that the beauty isn't only in the view before you—it's in the story of how you got there. No photograph can capture the mix of exhaustion, jubilation, relief, and awe that fills your chest.

The Emmaus disciples had their own summit moment. After a long, weary walk, they broke bread with the Stranger who had joined them—and suddenly the truth hit them like the sun cresting over a ridge and breaking through the clouds: it had been Jesus all along. "Were not our hearts burning within us…?" they say.

This generosity journey may have felt like that long climb—planning, praying, wrestling, adjusting your steps. There were moments of joy and moments of strain. But somewhere woven into it all was the still peaceful presence of Christ: in the stirring to give, in the stories that moved you, in the stillness where you finally listened.

The summit view isn't only about the amount you give—whether time, talent, energy, money, or focus. It's measured by the realization that you never walked alone. And it's marked by the deep warmth that comes when you recognize Christ's presence in every aspect of the journey. That is the heart set on fire.

Reflection: Looking back, where has your heart burned with the recognition of Christ on this journey?

SMALL GROUP GUIDE - WEEK 4

The Summit

Engaged listening, gratitude, shared load, hearts burning

Opening Check-In

What's one moment when you felt completely alive and present to God's presence?

Scripture Reading

Luke 24:13–35, Galatians 6:2; Hebrews 12:1–2

Insight & Reflection

Approaching the summit brings a mix of exhaustion and exhilaration. The disciples on the Emmaus road didn't know they were walking with Jesus—until he showed them his hands and their hearts burned within them. In generosity, the summit isn't only the view—it's recognizing God has been with you every step of the way.

Discussion Questions

1. How do you recognize God's presence in the midst of the climb?

2. Who helps you "carry the load" when the trail gets tough?

3. What spiritual legacy do you hope to leave behind?

Group Practice

Light a candle and allow time for silent reflection. Invite each person to name (aloud if comfortable) a community or ministry for whom their heart is beginning to burn.

Closing Prayer

Risen Christ, our constant Companion,
Open our eyes to recognize You on the road.
Kindle a fire in our hearts that cannot be contained.
As we share the load and the view from the mountaintop, may our lives reflect Your generosity and love to all we meet. May we be instruments of Thy peace, and may Thy will be done.
Amen

EPILOGUE — THE TRAIL AHEAD

If you've made it this far, you've taken a journey—not just through pages, but through heart-work. You've stopped along the way to lift your eyes from the ground beneath your feet, to look out at the bigger horizon, and to ask God, *"Where would You have me be in my giving and in my living?"*

The truth is, even after we've been reoriented, we can drift again. Trails twist. Fog rolls in. Life's weather changes—sometimes suddenly. You're met with a diagnosis, a job loss, a relationship strain. The same is true in our finances and volunteer service: what we planned to give may shift because of circumstances beyond our control.

But that's not failure. Faithfulness isn't about never adjusting; it's about realigning to God again and again. It's about remembering the cairns—those quiet markers that point us back when we've wandered. For the follower of Jesus, those markers are time, talent, treasure, and testimony—shaped by **gratitude, prayer, and service**. They guide us back to the heart of generosity and abundant living, even when the trail feels hard or the way forward isn't clear.

You may not be able to see the entire path from here. You may feel like the cloud cover is heavy over the view you hoped to reach. But remember: sometimes the most breathtaking vistas come only after a patient time of waiting, after the fog lifts, after the perseverance to stand still long enough for God to clear the way.

This devotional was never about guilt or hitting a number. It's been about movement—steady, prayerful steps toward a life shaped by God's generosity. It's about letting Him set your heading and walking in trust, knowing that every gift—whether given in abundance or in sacrifice—is part of Kingdom building work.

So take your next step. Keep your eyes on the horizon. And may every act of generosity become another marker on the trail leading you, and others, deeper into the joy of God's abundance.

THE GENEROSITY INCLINE

2 Corinthians 9:7–8

The Manitou Incline in Colorado is one of those climbs that looks impossible from the bottom—nearly 2,000 feet of gain in less than a mile, all on steep, uneven steps. From the trailhead, you can see the staircase stretching toward the clouds, daring you to try. Everyone starts in the same place, but they don't all finish in the same way. Some push all the way to the top in one go. Most pause for breaks along the way. Others stop at a midway turnout to head back down. Each climber and each climb is unique. Going part of the way is not failure—it's simply a different journey. You don't have to be a world-class mountaineer to enjoy the adventure—you simply have to be willing to take the next step.

Our giving works the same way. Each of us has a next step: maybe it's beginning to give regularly, moving toward a tithe, or giving beyond what we ever thought possible.

Of course, just as every climb has seasons when the path grows more challenging, sometimes, the generosity trail gets more difficult: a cancer diagnosis, a job loss, a family crisis. In those moments, your steps may look different—and that's okay. God doesn't call us to climb in guilt or fear, but as cheerful givers, stewarding each season in ways that honor Him. The important thing is to keep walking with God, letting Him guide how and where your generosity flows.

Generosity isn't one-dimensional. It's not only about the dollars we give or the hours we serve—it's both, and more. Scripture reminds us that our treasure and our time reveal what we value most. Money fuels ministry, expands impact, and sustains the daily work of the church. Time and presence, meanwhile, embody that generosity in flesh and blood—showing up with love, listening, serving, mentoring, and carrying burdens alongside others. Talents used and testimony given inspire and motivate others to get involved. When we give all of these, our faith becomes whole. We're not only resourcing the Kingdom; we're participating in it. Together, time, talents, treasures and testimony create a rhythm of generosity that changes lives—including our own.

FINDING YOUR NEXT STEP — THE COMPASS ROSE OF GENEROUS AND ABUNDANT LIVING

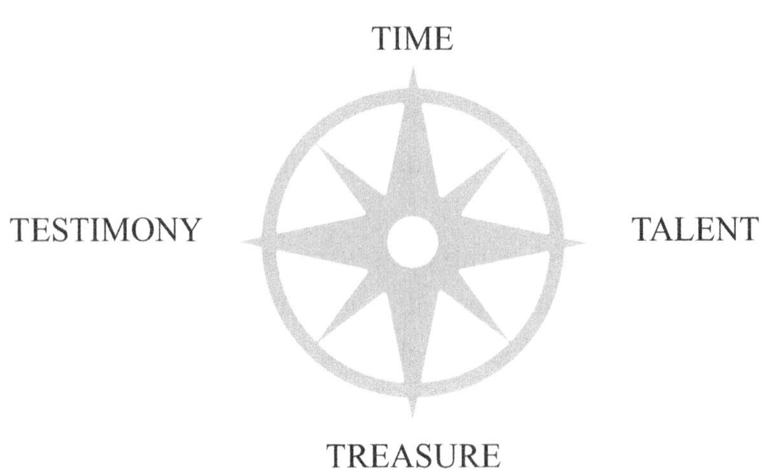

Like a compass points in four major directions, our generosity takes shape through time, talent, treasure, and testimony. Use these questions to discover where God is inviting your next step.

North – Time

- What percentage of my day and year do I give away in service to others?
- Am I carving out consistent time for ministry, presence, or simple acts of kindness?
- Where is God inviting me to reprioritize so I can be more available?

East – Talent

- Am I offering my skills, creativity, and passions to build others up and bless my community?
- How can I stretch my talents in new ways to glorify God?

South – Treasure

- What percentage of my resources do I give back to God?
- Am I giving first, or only out of what's left over?
- How is God inviting me to trust Him more fully with my finances?

West – Testimony

- How often am I telling the story of God's goodness in my life?
- Do I share gratitude and give credit to God openly in ways others can see, hear, and feel?
- What's one story I could share this week that might encourage someone else's faith?

GENEROSITY JOURNEY MILESTONES

Imagine your financial giving journey as a climb with rest points. Opportunities to soak in the experience along the way.

First Gift — The Tailhead

You've taken your first step by giving something—a starting point for the journey.

Occassional Giving — The Lower Steps

You give when you feel led or when a specific need arises.

Consistent Percentage Giving — Midway

You set a percentage of your income to give regularly.

Tithing (10%) — Upper Steps

You give a full tithe, and honor God with the first fruits of your income.

Extravagant Generosity — The Ridgeline

You give beyond the tithe, seeing all you have as God's and asking how it can bless others.

TIPS FOR SMALL GROUP LEADERS

Whether you've led groups for years or this is your first time, you are capable of creating a space that feels welcoming, unhurried, and real. Generosity is more than a theme—it's a way of living that makes safe and welcoming space for others to live abundantly into who God is forming them to be. Your role is to create the kind of atmosphere where that can happen.

Guiding Principles:

- Honor every voice. Make space for quieter people to share—and model vulnerability yourself.
- Don't force it. If someone is struggling, honor their honesty or silence.
- Stick to the timeframes you set. Each session is designed for 60–75 minutes. Adjust as needed.

Weekly Flow - each week includes:

1. Opening Check-In – Sets the tone. You don't need to teach a lesson. Simply guide the reflection.
2. Scripture Reading – Choose a few voices to read a passage to anchor your time together.
3. Insight & Reflection – Read aloud or summarize the week's theme using the trail metaphor and making a connection to something in your own life.
4. Discussion Questions – Use all if time allows, or pick the one that fits best for your group.
5. Group Activity – Keep it sacred and simple.
6. Closing Prayer

Tips for Group Discussion

- Let silence breathe. Sometimes people need a moment before they speak. Silently count to 6 if that helps you make space for them.
- Gently redirect if the group drifts off-topic.
- Be okay with "I don't know." Mystery is part of a generous spirit.

Generosity is a muscle. It can grow to impressive sizes, but it can also atrophy. People also go through seasons where their generosity muscle mass shifts. Also for some, this will come naturally. For others, it may feel like foreign territory. Be patient. Encourage consistency. Trust that God will meet people where they are. You don't need to teach a lesson. Simply facilitate reflection. Let scripture and the Spirit do the heavy lifting. Your job is to create space and invite connection.

THE FIRST GATHERING

Thank you for saying yes to leading!

Your willingness to guide others through this journey brings the content to life in ways that couldn't happen without you. I hope that in leading you will discover an extra portion of divine wisdom, abundance, and insight.

What follows are some resources to invite others to open their hearts as you have—and to make space for one another along the way. May you feel inspired, supported, and surprised by grace.

I am cheering you on!

Opening Blessing (Leader or Group in Unison)

We gather, not because we have it all together,
but because God's generous spirit invites us in.

We come with open hearts,
Ready to give, ready to receive,
Ready to be surprised by grace.

May this be a safe space for truth,
A brave space for growth,
And a holy space for experiencing divine abundance.

We begin this journey, side by side—
As companions in the pursuit of a generous and abundant life.
Amen.

Group Covenant

To Be Discussed and Affirmed Together

As we begin this journey, we commit to:

- Show Up With Honesty - We don't have to pretend. An abundant life grows stronger when it's real.
- Listen With Care - We give each person the gift of full attention—no fixing, just presence.
- Honor What's Shared - Stories stay here. Trust grows here.
- Embrace the Practice - We'll try each week's group activity—even if it feels awkward at first.
- Encourage One Another - We celebrate progress, not perfection. We call out goodness in each other.
- Seek God Together - Through scripture, conversation, and silence, we'll make space for God's generous and abundant spirit to shape us.

Group Leader Prompt:

"Are we willing to commit to these intentions as we journey together?" (Pause for nods, affirmations, or spoken agreement.)

Note: Whether you've led groups for years or this is your first time, you don't need to be perfect—you simply need to be present. A generous and abundant life grows best in safe and honest spaces. Your role is to create the kind of atmosphere where that can happen.

FREE WORSHIP RESOURCES

Want More?

Additional Devotional and Sermon Series Resources are available for FREE online.

Vile Methods sermon series come with a *free downloadable PDF* full of worship and discipleship tools you can actually use. Resource packs include:

- Children's Lessons
- Calls to worship, opening & unison prayers
- Song suggestions & video ideas
- Promo content for your church & community

No paywalls. No fine print. Just practical tools for raw, Spirit-led ministry.

Download now at www.VileMethods.com

RESOURCES

Bibles & Biblical Reference Tools

Holy Bible, New International Version. Grand Rapids, MI: Zondervan, 2011.

Holy Bible, New Revised Standard Version. Nashville: Thomas Nelson, 1989.

OakTree Software. *Accordance Bible Software.* 2009.

Strong, James. *The Exhaustive Concordance of the Bible.* Nashville: Abingdon Press, 1890.

Journals, Articles, and Studies

[1] Gallup. "A Kinder World Is a Happier One." *Gallup News*, 2024. https://news.gallup.com/opinion/gallup/657998/kinder-world-happier-one.aspx.

[2] Harvard T.H. Chan School of Public Health. "Kindness Linked to Better Physical Health and Longevity." *Harvard News*, 2024. https://www.health.harvard.edu/staying-healthy/the-healing-power-of-kindness.

[3] Harvard Health Publishing. "The Healing Power of Kindness." *Harvard Health Blog*, 2023. https://journals.sagepub.com/doi/abs/10.1177/0963721413512503.

[4] Dunn, E., Aknin, L., Norton, M. "Does Spending Money on Others Promote Happiness?" *Journal of Consumer Psychology* / Harvard Business School, 2008, 2014. https://www.hbs.edu/ris/Publication Files/Does Spending Money on Others Promote Happiness_acc24566-c7c9-4f03-b918-9d25628264c8.pdf

[5] Pew Research Center. "How Highly Religious Americans' Lives Are Different." *Pew Research*, 2016. https://www.pewresearch.org/short-reads/2016/04/12/how-highly-religious-americans-lives-are-different-from-others/.

[6] Lewis Center for Church Leadership. "Church Giving and Worship Attendance Trends." *Leading Ideas*, 2024. https://www.churchleadership.com/leading-ideas/church-giving-and-worship-attendance-trends-an-in-depth-interview-with-joe-park/.

[7] Gallup. "Global Generosity: The World Felt Less Charitable in 2024." *Gallup Poll*, 2024. https://news.gallup.com/poll/657200/global-generosity-world-felt-less-charitable-2024.aspx.

[8] Notre Dame. *Science of Generosity* Project, generosityresearch.nd.edu. https://generosityresearch.nd.edu/.

[9] Salamon, Maureen. *The Healing Power of Kindness. Harvard Health Publishing*, April 1, 2025.

[10] Jansen, Jim. *The Civic and Community Engagement of Religiously Active Americans.* Pew Research Center (Internet & American Life Project), December 23, 2011.

Wilderness Navigation & Education

[11] Wells, Darran. *Wilderness Navigation.* Stackpole Books, 2005.

NOTES ON LANGUAGE AND TRANSLATION

Throughout this book, I have drawn from various biblical translations, including the **New International Version (NIV)** and the **New Revised Standard Version (NRSV)**. Unless otherwise noted, quotations are from the NIV. However, in some cases, I have provided my own translations from the original **Hebrew and Greek texts** where it better reflects the narrative, theological, or poetic emphasis of this work.

Translation Considerations

The translation choices in this book are meant to **enhance accessibility, preserve theological depth, and illuminate biblical metaphors** in a way that encourages deeper engagement. Where language is traditionally ambiguous or open to interpretation, I have sought to retain its richness while ensuring clarity for a modern audience.

Several key considerations shaped my approach:

1. **Theological Emphasis:** Certain words or phrases have been rendered with **theological weight in mind**, highlighting **themes of covenant, redemption, and transformation**.
2. **Metaphoric Integrity:** Biblical metaphors often lose their impact when flattened into rigid translations. Where applicable, I have **preserved the poetic nature of the text** to retain its literary and theological resonance.

3. **Inclusive and Expansive Language:** Biblical language is deeply relational, and this book **aims to reflect the breadth of God's love and justice**. Where appropriate, I have used inclusive language that **remains faithful to the original intent while ensuring clarity** for contemporary readers.
4. **Historical and Cultural Context:** Scripture was written in specific cultural settings, and certain terms carry **nuances that modern readers may miss**. Some renderings reflect insights from **historical scholarship and biblical studies** to **unveil the deeper meaning of the text**.

Names and Pronouns for God

The Bible describes God in **a variety of ways**, using **masculine, feminine,** and **neutral imagery**. While **God transcends human gender**, language inherently shapes how we understand the divine. In this book:

- **I have retained masculine pronouns for God** because **they are the most familiar to many readers** and reflect how the Bible has traditionally been translated. This choice is not intended to limit or define God but rather to ensure accessibility while allowing room for deeper reflection. Additionally, pronouns like **He** help maintain the **personal nature of God found throughout Scripture**, a closeness that coincides with the **mystery and grandeur of God's transcendent nature**.
- **The Holy Spirit is sometimes referred to with feminine or neutral language**, as the original Hebrew (**ruach**) is grammatically **feminine**, and the Greek (**pneuma**) is

neuter. These variations remind us that **the Spirit transcends conventional gender categories** and has been described in ways that emphasize both **nurturing** and **powerful** aspects of divine presence.

A Living and Breathing Story

The Bible is not a static text but **a living story**, inviting us into its rhythms, themes, and unfolding revelation. My goal is not simply to translate words but to **illuminate meaning**—to help readers **encounter the grand narrative of the Bible in a way that speaks to both heart and mind**.

For those interested in deeper study, I encourage you to compare translations, explore the **Hebrew and Greek nuances**, and wrestle with the text in **community, conversation, and prayer**.

FIELD NOTES

"The only gift is a portion of thyself." Ralph Waldo Emerson

FIELD NOTES

"When you are in the will of God, it ceases to be a duty and becomes a delight." E. Stanley Jones

FIELD NOTES

"Twenty years from now you will be more disappointed by the things you didn't do than by the ones you did do. So throw off the bowlines... Explore. Dream. Discover." Mark Twain

ABOUT THE AUTHOR

Rev. Dr. Tyler Kaufmann is an ordained minister in the United Methodist Church. He received his Master of Divinity from Drew Theological School in Madison, NJ. He received his Doctor of Ministry from Portland Seminary in Newberg, OR, where he studied Semiotics, Church, and Culture alongside the academic field of creativity research under Rev. Dr. Leonard Sweet.

Tyler is currently serving as the Senior Pastor of Leawood United Methodist Church in Leawood, Kansas. He is also the founder of Vile Methods, a ministry focused on encouraging and equipping people to “wake the dead” and “be more vile” for the sake of the Gospel.

Whether rock climbing, hiking national parks with his son Theo, or hosting creative Bible studies in unexpected places, Tyler is always searching for signs of grace in the wild that can transform ordinary moments into extraordinary encounters of the sacred.

To Learn More Visit,

www.vilemethods.com

Resources and Inspiration for Innovative Ministry

Made in the USA
Monee, IL
29 September 2025

30520001R00049